AWAKEN YOUR GODDESS AND DIVINE FEMININE POWERS

WORKBOOK

Healing, Transformation, and Reconnection to Your Body, Voice, Intuition, Womb, and Self–love

Anastasia Spencer

AWAKEN YOUR GODDESS AND DIVINE FEMININE POWERS

ISBN: (Paperback - 979-8-9883157-8-0)
Library of Congress Control Number (LCCN) - 2023911109

First Edition: May 2023

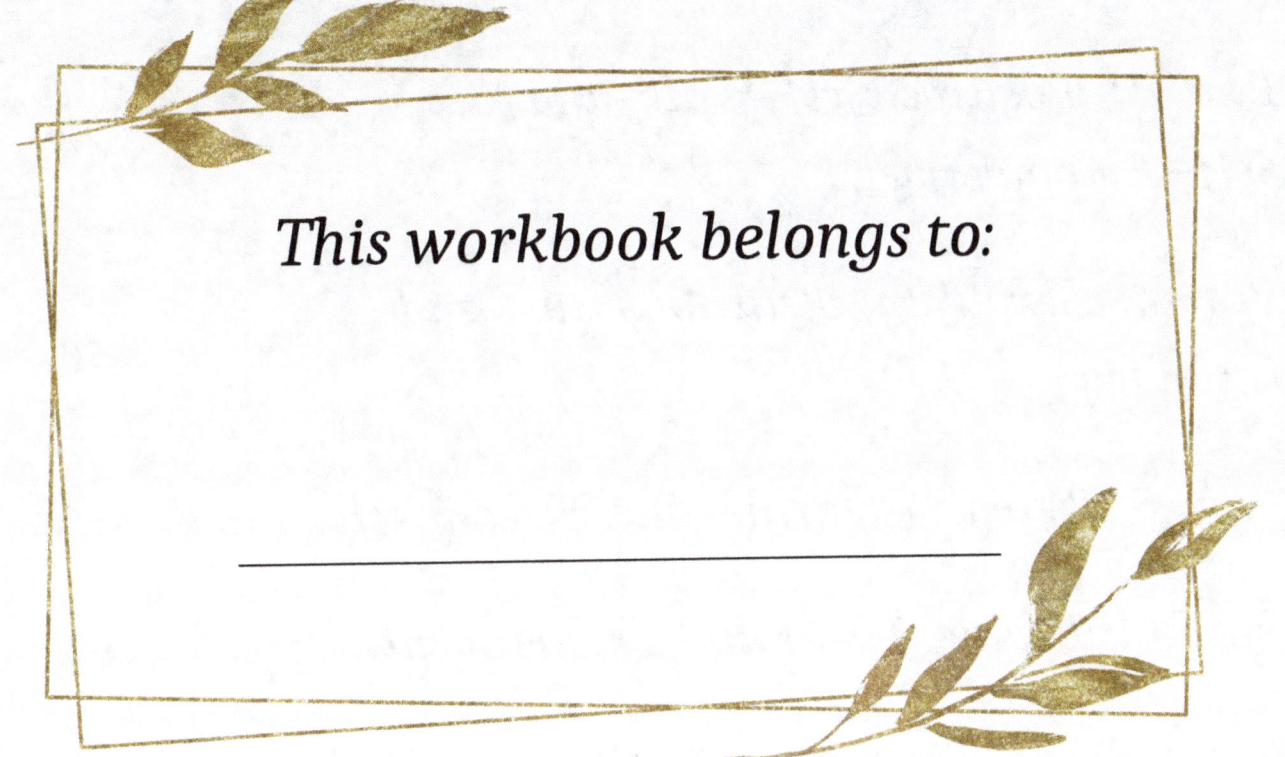

This workbook belongs to:

_____

Table of Contents

Welcome to You!
Divine, Beautiful, and Powerful Goddess!

I am so grateful you said YES to yourself. If you are holding this book, then this sacred medicine is meant for you. This workbook is designed to guide you through the journey of transformation, so you can discover your strengths, fall in love with your body, celebrate yourself, learn how to embrace all emotions and become whole. Did you know that your subconscious mind permanently stores everything that ever happened to you and your subconscious controls 95% of your day? Only you have the power to transform limiting beliefs, past, and trauma. It is never too early or too late to experience the deepest truth of who you are.

How to connect to Divine Feminine Power and Inner Goddess?

- Find the courage to face your fears, old patterns, and stories and break through the energy that confines you and holds you back from being a pure expression of divine light, grace, and love.
- Witness your emotions and uncomfortable feelings. Accept, love, and give a voice to your emotions and feelings.

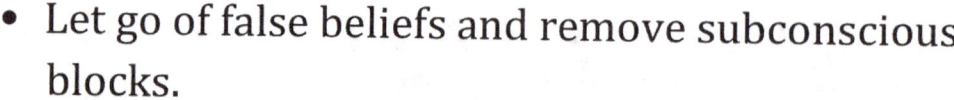

- Let go of false beliefs and remove subconscious blocks.
- Let go of your victimhood story and right/wrong models.
- Change your patterns of behaviors and reactions.
- Welcome all soul fragments and parts of you that were disconnected with full acceptance and love.
- Clear unhealthy energies and reconnect with your sacred womb.
- Honor your body as a sacred temple of love.
- Set healthy and clear boundaries with others.
- Speak your inner truth to yourself and others from the space of strength.
- Allow powerful vibrations of passion, desire, pleasure, and pure joy to flow freely through your body.
- Take new actions, commit to yourself, and let go of the need for people to like you.
- Express yourself freely, find your voice, and let go of the fear of being too much or not enough.
- Surrender to your own unfolding and embrace the unknown.
- Learn self-respect and self-love without compromise.
- Choose high-vibrational, positive, and empowering words for yourself and others.
- Do what makes you feel happy and radiant.

Empowering Declaration to Yourself

It is time to fully embrace my **Divine Goddess Powers!**
I love and honor myself with every fiber of my being.
I breathe deeply and connect with my body.
I have the keys to change my life!
I embrace uncomfortable feelings, emotions, and memories.
I give a voice to them and allow myself to grow.
I am a pure expression of Divine Feminine energy!

I am willing to...

_____

_____

I am ready to...

_____

_____

I am calling into my life...

_____

_____

I invite you to read those statements out loud 3 times. Repetition is where the magic happens. Welcome all emotions and feelings that arise and surrender fully to this transformational journey.

Awareness + Learning + Growth = Healing and Expansion

Let's begin...

Activation of the Healing and Transformational Energies:

I invite you to enter into the Sacred Gateway of the Divine Feminine within you.

Feel the vibrations of love that flow through every cell and every fiber of your being.

Allow yourself to go even deeper, sending your awareness to your sacred heart, a place of birth of your Enlighted Self, a new blueprint of your life.

Enter into a new level of awareness of the light within you.

Feel your heart expanding more and more.

Your channel is clear.

The earth plane is ready for this initiation on what love truly is and how the vibrations of love can transform everything.

You play an important role in that process.

But first, let's restore your connection to the inner light.

Become aware of expanded light pulsating in your body.

You were guided to go through this powerful transformational journey because your Soul knows that you are ready, and you have been calling consciously or unconsciously the transformational vibrations that are offered here in this inner journey.

Relax even deeper into the process that is activated within you.

Heal shattered pieces of your child self and soul fragments.

Return back to wholeness.

Allow healing, clearing, and awakening energies to flow through your entire being.

Activate passion, aliveness, and soul purpose.

Let go of the limited 3rd-dimensional story.

Feel inner yearning to move forward into new life, a new way of living, and your higher vibrational, limitless, and full potential self.

Step fully into **Divine Feminine Power and Inner Goddess** vibrations; breathe it in deeply and let it flow through your essence and become fully the light that you always have been.

I invite you to set your personal intention for this sacred journey.

Setting Intention:

An intention is an energetic signal that you send to the Universe. When you set your intention, make sure that it is emotionally charged and that there is power behind it. Be specific, clear, write it down, and read it out loud at least 3 times. Once you set your intention, the Universe will help you fulfill your intention. If you are vibrationally aligned with your intention, it would happen instantly or very easily. However, if you are not vibrationally aligned with it, then you will be guided through the journey of letting go, clearing, and creating space for those new energies. You need to face this step with gratitude and openness to let go so the Universe can help you to manifest your intention.

Clear Intention + Elevated Emotion = CHANGE

You can create the life of your dreams. Everything is possible. You just have to believe and embrace your inner power!

I FOLLOW MY Heart

Part 1: Healing Transformation

Invocation of Transformation Energies:

I am calling upon Healing Light, pure vibrations of Love and Transformation. I command to be free of low-vibration energies that trap me in the field of pain, suffering, trauma, old patterns, and keep me from my soul evolution and pure love. I choose to restore the connection to my Higher Self and the Higher Vibrational essence of my Divine Soul. I am the love code carrier. I am a pure channel of Light. I am loving awareness. I AM THAT I AM. And so it is.

AWARENESS:

Old Story of Early Childhood: Honor and witness your own old stories and childhood memories. What emotions, feelings, memories, and experiences did you choose to let go of?

Old Story of Adult Experiences: Honor and witness your own old stories and adult memories. What emotions, feelings, memories, and experiences did you choose to let go of?

Soul Fragments Recollection: What parts of you need to return back to you? Was it part of you that you gave away to others, or was it disconnected in your childhood or adulthood? Write down everything that comes to you. It can be a color, word, name, image, emotion, etc.

- Place your hands on your heart.
- Breathe in – open your arms; energy goes out to collect all missing soul fragments.
- Breathe out – guide your hands back to your heart to bring all soul fragments back to wholeness, back to yourself.

Witnessing Your Emotions: Identify what emotions you feel strongly. Be honest and truthful with yourself. How does an emotion make your body feel? Be in a state of openness for anything that arises and stay present with whatever your mind, emotions, and body are processing. Give a voice to your emotions. Ask each emotion what message it has for you. Be open to receiving a message in any form, including a word, color, sensation, or vision. Write down your self-reflections.

Witnessing Your Own Inner Judge and Critic: Become aware of your own words, thoughts, and actions that disempower you and foster self-abuse and self-judgment. Remember that you are using your immense power against yourself. It is time to transform disempowering inner judgmental and critical energies. Write down at least 3 examples of your inner judge and critic (relationships, career, family, body, etc.). How can you transform into self-empowerment?

Revealing Your Inner Truth, False Core Beliefs, Heart-Armoring Beliefs: Identify false beliefs that run your life and tell you negative things. Unconsciously, you might constantly exist on survival high alert for rejection, pain, suffering, separation, abandonment, etc. The false beliefs and attachments that are stored in your body limit your true expression and joy. Also, they rule your life and define your reality. What beliefs you would like to let go of?

Old Ways of Power: Power is not sought after from outside, but rather is patiently cultivated from within. Does your strength come from how you look, how much money you have, how well you take care of others? How do you define your power and self-worth?

Become Aware of Coping Strategies

Over time, we create a coping strategy to feel a sense of safety and security. However, it is just a temporary patch for something that needs attention, healing, and transformation.

Here are the main coping strategies. Identify which one applies to you. It can be one strategy or multiple strategies.

- **Controller** - Feel safe when you are in control of your life. You have a tendency to manage other's emotions, choices, and decisions through subtle or blatant domination or manipulation.

- **Distractor** - Feel safe by staying busy and checked out. Instead of feeling your feelings and facing discomfort, you tend to distract yourself with social media, video games, doing projects/hobbies, talking to friends, watching TV, shopping, etc. Your energy is so scattered that is hard to focus and create what you want in life.

- **Isolator** - Feel safe when you are alone and hide. You have a tendency to constrict your own energy and choices.

- **Pleaser** - It makes you feel accepted, loved, and safe when you are helping others and making them feel happy. You feel lost when you are not caretaking or helping.

Witness your strategy: How does it affect your life? Are you ready to transform your core strategies into healthy vibrations?

Discover Energy Leaks in Your Life: Catch every moment you are aware of the energy leaks. It could be unhealthy attachments to people, addictions, situations, emotions, patterns, self-lies, etc. Without realizing it, it affects your energy level, health, personal life, career, and romantic relationships.

Write down all energy leaks that you are aware of…

Invocation of Healing Energies:

I am calling upon Higher Powers, Divine Healing Light, Mother Earth, Cosmic Mother and Father, Angels, Archangels, High-Vibrational Spirit Guides, and Soul Essence of (Your Name).

I am asking for your blessings, guidance, protection, support, and healing energies.

I am asking for your help to remove all impurities, negative thought forms, parasites, negative entities, and disharmony on all levels, dimensions, and realities.

Clear all trauma, past memories, energetic and karmic cords, negative entities, thought forms, and impurities.

Assist to restore all layers of existence, physical, emotional, mental, energetic, and spiritual.

Help to restore the High–Vibrational Divine Blueprint and Divine Soul Energies of (Your Name).

I am asking for your assistance to help (Your Name) to awaken her inner light, soul purpose, and deep awareness of herself.

I, (Your Name), am grateful for all soul lessons. Now, I choose to transmute and transform all energies, vibrations, thoughts, and actions that are not in alignment with the high–vibrational energy of love and light.

I choose to fully heal my body and mind and restore all soul fragments. I choose to embrace all my emotions and thoughts that are not in alignment with my pure essence by transmuting and transforming all those energies back to light.

I am grateful for this precious gift—Life beyond time and space.

I choose to fully embrace life. Thank you, Mother Earth, for your sacred invitation to be here and now.

From this moment, I choose to create consciously, emanate high-vibrational energies, think positively, and be an example to others of the miracle of spontaneous healing.

I am Divine Light, Love, and High-Vibrational Energy of Creation.

I choose to always radiate my pure soul essence and my bright inner light.

I am Light.
I am Divine.
I am that I am.
And so be it!

FORGIVENESS:

Step out of the victimhood energies and into your Divine Feminine power. It is possible through awareness, compassion, and forgiveness. To complete your soul lessons, you need to become aware of what those experiences wanted to teach you. Then, set free the person/situation/experience with compassion and forgiveness and detach yourself completely physically, emotionally, mentally, and energetically.

Take time to write down your soul lessons and your reflections.

Person/People toward whom you feel resentment and make you feel angry:

Person/People that you hate or people who hate you:

Person/People who hurt you or people who have been hurt by you:

Invocation of Compassion and Forgiveness:

Thank you for helping me awaken my pure essence and remembrance of who I am. I am loving awareness, pure consciousness, and love.

From this moment, I choose to forgive everyone who has ever hurt or harmed me, consciously or unconsciously, in this lifetime or any other, in this universe, dimension, plane, level of existence, or any other.

I offer them loving awareness, grace, and compassion.
I ask for forgiveness for everything I have ever done to hurt or harm another, consciously or unconsciously, in this lifetime or any other, in this universe, dimension, plane, level of existence, or any other.

I forgive myself for everything I have ever done, consciously or unconsciously, in this lifetime or any other, in this universe, dimension, plane, level of existence, or any other.

I accept loving awareness, grace, and compassion.

I set myself free. All restrictions, debts, and karma are erased and dissolve back into the pure light.
From this moment, I choose to be pure light and loving awareness. I AM THAT I AM.

I am ready to forgive…

◆ ---

◆ ---

◆ ---

◆ ---

◆ ---

I am calling PEACE, HARMONY, and PURE LOVE into my life!

I invite you to read those statements out loud 3 times. Repetition is where the magic happens. Welcome all emotions and feelings that arise and surrender fully to this transformational journey.

ACTION:

Commit to You: Release old habits of the need to please others, co-dependency, seeking validations, saying Yes when you meant No, and a need to be constantly saved. Speak your truth to yourself and others from a place of love and strength. Become aware of other habits that are not high-vibrational. Write down new habits and how you choose to commit to yourself.

Connect to Your Passions and Desires: What are you passionate about? What do you desire to create? Release all fearful should, what ifs, and don'ts. Collect your scattered energy. Connect to your warrior energy, which is a combination of focus, dedication, purpose, and determination. Also, connect to your creative flow energy, which is love, pleasure, passion, and wisdom. Dream big and follow your passion!

Claiming Your Strength and Power: Write down what you really want for yourself. Not what your victim wants, or what your judge wants, but your highest vision and purpose is for yourself. What do you want your intimate relationships to look like? What do you want your career to look like? What do you want the relationships with your family and friends to look like? What do you want your free time to look like?

Now, read this declaration statement out loud with intention and power!

Declaration to Myself:

I don't require any low-vibrational stories to be part of my reality. I choose to let go, to remove it so it no longer continues in this lifetime or future. Anything and everything that doesn't allow me to create with ease, I destroy. Clear it.

I choose to return old stories back to the library. I choose to archive old stories that are not high vibrations so they no longer repeat on this planet.

Those stories are not part of me anymore. Everything that weighed me down is GONE NOW!

NOW, I CREATE new stories that I want to experience. I create with ease and grace a brand-new book with new pictures, experiences, and people.

Creating a New Story of Life: Become aware of your old story and take responsibility for your old story. Make conscious actions and free yourself. Write down your new story that is charged with high-vibrational energies of love, inner power, strength, peace, passion, and desire.

Part 2: Process of Loving Yourself

Come up with an adjective for each letter of your name. Write it down. Sit in front of the mirror, look into your eyes, and say each adjective out loud 3 times. Notice how you feel and what emotions, visions, or messages come up for you.

Example: ANASTASIA
A- Amazing
N- Nice
A- Aware
S- Special
T- Thoughtful
A- Ancient
S- Strong
I- Immortal
A- Affectionate

YOUR NAME

Self-empowerment: Identify and write down your unique gifts, strengths, and talents.

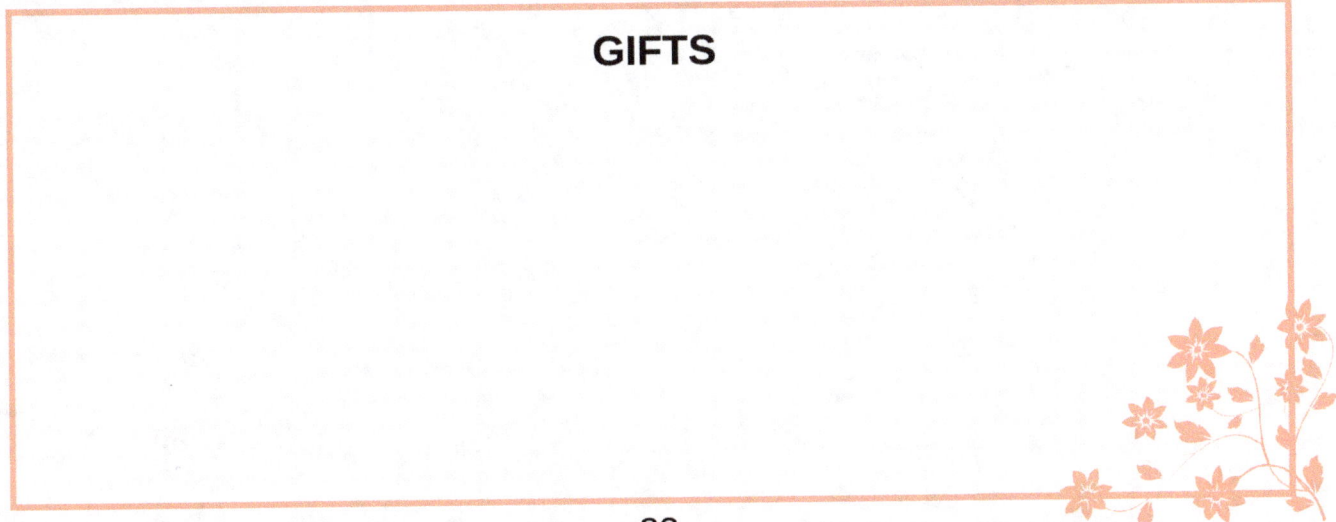

GIFTS

STRENGTHS

TALENTS

Healthy Boundary Setting: Write down what would your healthy boundary look like in your personal life, career, family, intimate relationships, and among friends. Always remember to express your truth, prioritize yourself, be authentic, state your needs, and just be you.

Self-Love in Relationships: Write down how self-love shows up in your relationships: negative concept vs. positive change.

Body Language Makes a Difference: Confident vs. Insecure
Become aware of how your body responds to certain triggers, situations, experiences, people, patterns, etc. You might notice unnecessary tension, pain, incorrect posture, unnecessary giggling, coughing, etc. Write down what you notice.

Love Language: Ask your body: What do you want more of? What do you want less of? Go beneath the habits and quick fixes to listen to your body's wisdom and depth. How do you nurture, nourish, and express love to yourself?

LOVE and Gratitude Letter to Myself

Dear_____(your name here),

_____

_____

_____

_____

_____

_____

_____

_____

_____

_____

_____

Love _____(your name here)

LOVE and Gratitude Letter to My Body

Dear Body _____,

Love _____ *(your name here)*

Self-Worth Tracker: When you love yourself, you have an appreciation for your own worth or value. Create new healthy and powerful habits for building your self-worth. Write down any observations that you become aware of on a daily basis.
For example, healthy boundaries, body language, self-empowerment, love language, positive words about yourself, and self-love practice. Notice any disempowering actions and words, then transmute them to empowering self-worth practice.

Weekly Calendar

Monday	Tuesday	Wednesday	Thursday	Friday	Saturday	Sunday

Part 3: Positive Self-Talk, and Empowerment

Invocation of Transformation:

I am (for example, SAFE) _____

I am willing to destroy and uncreate ALL, NEVER, ALWAYS

It doesn't serve a purpose anymore.

I choose to uncreate views, beliefs, judgments, and perceptions.

Clearing through all times, space, dimensions, realities, parallel universes, multiverses, everything known and unknown, said and unsaid, willingly acknowledged and not acknowledged.

Inhale and exhale, releasing it from the field

I am (for example, SAFE) _____NOW

Rewrite How You Think and Talk

Your body is very intelligent technology; your thoughts and beliefs are the software; your life is the printout of the two. Change the software, rewrite the beliefs, and change your life. From this moment, choose positive words and speak kindly to yourself.

Read those statements or your own out loud at least 3 times before going to bed or when you wake up.

- *I choose myself first*
- *I express myself freely*
- *I allow myself to give and receive pleasure*
- *I am creative*
- *I love my body*
- *I love myself*
- *I accept myself*
- *I am strong, graceful, and full of light*
- *I surrender to the flow*
- *I honor and express my femininity*
- *I speak my truth*
- *I effortlessly create beautiful things*
- *I am one with the Earth*
- *I attract abundance*
- *I am whole*
- *I honor my sensuality and sexuality*
- *I am Divine*

- *I AM*
- *I am sacred*
- *I make empowering choices*
- *I shine my light and radiance*
- *I manifest my dreams with ease and grace*
- *I trust my intuition*
- *I am worthy of love and all blessings*
- *I am free to be me*
- *I am grounded, safe, and protected*
- *I am radiant and full of light and love*
- *I set healthy boundaries*
- *I am confident*
- *I do what I love*
- *I choose to live life to the fullest*
- *I create my own happiness*
- *I am unique, and I am proud of myself*
- *I am a powerful creator*
- *I am the expression of Divine Feminine energy*
- *I follow my Soul purpose*
- *I choose flow, ease, and grace*
- *I forgive myself and others*
- *I fully embrace my Divine Feminine powers*

- *I breathe deeply and connect to my body*
- *I am grateful for this life*
- *I am magic*
- *I am special*
- *I am a Divine channel of Light*
- *I let life fully that I deserve*
- *I am strong*
- *I am centered*
- *I am courageous*

Create Your Own Affirmations:

- I am…
- I have…
- I feel…

Part 4: Sexuality, Relationships, and Intimacy

Witnessing Your Own Beliefs about Sacred Sexuality and Sensuality:

What limiting beliefs do you have about sexuality and sensuality? Write them down. Release old stories that you were taught about sexuality. "It is dangerous. It is shameful. It is not spiritual. I will get hurt. I will be rejected. I am too old for that. It is dirty and sinful." It is blocking you from manifesting your life. Honor where you are, and allow yourself to shift to your growth zone.

Reclaim Your Sacred Sexuality and Sensuality: Sexual energy is a potent force of nature that flows through everything and everyone. Your sacred sexuality is sacred, powerful, and one of the Divine's gifts. Sexual energy can be expressed in many ways, including creativity and passion. As you reclaim your sexuality for yourself, you will become more confident. You would get clear about what you want and what you don't want. You will find your voice, self-respect, and lose your fear of being too much or not enough.

Notice if you were triggered in any place reading this. What is your mind saying to you? Explore your reactions. What does sacred sexuality and sensuality mean to you? What brings you a sense of sacred sensuality and pleasure?

Healing Statement:

I am one with Life Force, and creative energy flows freely through me. I fully accept my sacred sexuality and sensuality. It is my birthright. I am not the patterns and beliefs that I inherited from my ancestors, parents, society, and upbringing. I love my body and it is safe to feel good. I give full permission to myself to feel passion, pleasure, sensations, and emotions. It is safe for me to explore my own temple and sacred sanctuary within me.

I love and embrace all vulnerability and sensitivity that comes from being a woman. I am safe to give and receive love. My feminine essence is powerful. I declare that this is my truth, and I accept it as so.

How did your last relationship end? What lesson did you learn from that relationship? Each person in our life is for a reason. They help us to grow and evolve.

Think about your last two intimate relationships. What were the major patterns and lessons?

Releasing Past Lovers

- Connect with his/her energy in your heart and womb
- Set intention: only pure love and pure gratitude
- What soul lessons did you learn with your past lover?

Place your hand on your heart and your womb. Connect to your inner self.

Say out loud this statement:
(Name), I love you, your heart, and your spirit without any attachments
I am thankful for all the soul lessons that I learned
I choose to release you from my energy field, womb, heart, emotional, and physical bodies with love and gratitude.
Breathe into your heart and womb. Breathe out, release your hands from your body.
Feel the stillness, harmony, and peace.

Healing Statement:

I am willing to release the need for relationships that don't nourish and support me. I am not the patterns and beliefs that I inherited from my ancestors, parents, society, and upbringing. I honor my own unique self. I choose to invite sacred, loving, and long-lasting relationships. I give full permission to myself to experience intimate love. I am worthy of love. I am love. I AM THAT I AM. So it is.

What are you looking for in relationships? Describe in detail and charged with emotion. How would you feel to manifest your ideal relationship? Believe in yourself. You can manifest love and a partner of your dreams.

Part 5: Womb Clearing and Reconnection

- Explore what energies, emotions, and sensations are held in your womb from past experiences
- Cleanse your womb of tension, limitation, and heavy emotions
- Plant a seed of healing light within your womb
- Reconnect to your womb and wisdom from within

What negative things have you been taught about your womb or menstrual cycle by society, your mother, sisters, friends, and others? The womb is not a place to store fear and pain. It is a sacred place to create and give birth to life.

What negative things do you feel about your womb in general? How would you like to feel toward your womb instead? How do you feel about the process of menstruation? Of childbirth? What negative words or feelings come up for you when you think of these things?

Coming Home to Yourself: The womb is a sacred space where we connect to mystery, Mother Earth, Death/Birth, and Rebirth. Through the womb, we can reconnect to Source, infinite potential, and the effortless, natural ability to create. Do you feel numbness, resistance, fear, disconnect, trauma, hurt, or pain in your womb area?

Reconnect with Your Womb: Place your hands on your belly and lower abdomen. Take a moment to listen and feel. What would you like to say to your womb? What would you like to thank your womb for today?

Part 6: Divine Feminine Embodiment

When you embody your Divine Feminine energy, you step into the power, abundance, free-flowing creativity, and aligned manifestations. Allow yourself to reconnect with the inner wisdom stored within your body so you can emerge as the radiant goddess you were born to be.

Choose one strength/quality from the list that you desire to step into embodying more fully:

- Presence
- Awareness
- Rest
- Stillness
- Being
- Flowing
- Free
- Spontaneous
- Allowing
- Surrender
- Release
- Intuitive
- Compassion
- Love
- Expressive
- Wise
- Receiving
- Nurturing
- Gentle
- Comfort
- Patient
- Softness

How can you step into fully embodying this quality or strength? What, if anything, is holding you back from doing so?

What must change in your heart, mind, and actions to embody this quality or strength more fully?

Healing Statement:

From this moment, I am open to embracing and embodying Divine Feminine strength [insert name of strength_____] more fully within myself. I welcome experiences to strengthen and solidify this for myself with ease and joy. I choose to fully cultivate and express within myself the strength of [insert name of strength_____].

Part 7: The Power of Gratitude

Gratitude changes everything. The gratitude practice is a powerful tool to manifest your dreams, goals, and intentions. It intensifies energies, changes your mindset, and increases joy.

What are you grateful for? Write down at least 10 things and use as much detail as possible. Connect to your grateful heart. Feel it in your body when you say out loud what you are grateful for.

I am **GRATEFUL** for…

70

I **THANK MYSELF** for…

Part 8: Empowered Goddess Self-Love Ritual

Create a daily self-love ritual for an abundant, healthy, and balanced life. Let it be your creative way to express gratitude, care, and love for yourself and your body. Commit to the practice of sacred ritual by starting each day with this nurturing, loving, and high-vibrational energy. What brings you the most joy, pleasure, relaxation, and happiness? Be specific as possible.

I CELEBRATE YOU, YOUR POWER, STRENGTH, AND COURAGE TO DIVE DEEP INTO THIS TRANSFORMATIONAL JOURNEY.

I invite you to continue your self-mastery and self-love practice!

Want to go deeper into the practice of self-love and embrace fully your sacred sexuality and sensuality?

Are you ready to say YES to the powerful life force and wisdom of your body? I lead this deep sacred container for sisters who are ready to remember their soul's power, beauty, sensuality, and love in the purest form. Feel empowered within, honored and respected, and divinely connected to your powers. Embrace Divine Feminine body, voice, intuition, and power to speak truth, and show up fully and authentically. Connect to your menstrual cycles and the cyclic rhythm of the moon, the seasons, and the wheel.

In this sacred container, we would learn Divine Feminine tantric energy medicine and practice deep embodiment tools to assist in your awakening of inner powers, kundalini energy, and connecting with your body and sensuality on a deeper level.

EXPLORE OTHER OFFERINGS AND COURSES:
WWW.PORTALOFREBIRTH.COM

About the Author:

Anastasia Spencer is a gifted intuitive healer, hypnotherapist, yogi, spiritual coach, psychic, medium, animal spirit communicator, multidimensional channeler, motivational speaker, holistic doula, and conscious educator.

Anastasia empowers individuals through intuitive guidance, healing, and education. She has conducted thousands of readings and healing sessions for clients all over the world both online and in person. She helps souls tap into their own psychic abilities and teaches about subconscious mind reprogramming, transcendental meditation, self-healing, and tools for ascension. Anastasia channels the Cosmic Light, Messages from Source, Spirit Guides, Angels, Archangels, Extra-Terrestrial Beings, Mother Gaia, Loved Ones, and Pets.

She helps souls clear any dark spirit attachments, blockages, and energetic parasites. Anastasia travels into the akashic records of your soul by accessing your past lives and existence on other planets, stars, and dimensions.

Anastasia is honored to be on this planet to help others remember their true essence and guide them through the deep awakening journey to realize their highest potential, activate and understand their Soul gifts, and free themselves from limiting beliefs and obstacles.

Anastasia can be reached through her website at www.portalofrebirth.com or via email at portalofrebirth@gmail.com

Blessings and Gratitude
May love and peace be your guides,
Joy and Happiness be your friends,
And every breath be a reminder of who you are!
Namaste!